D1621489

# ABC CHARLOTTE

Written by Christina Berkau Pope
Illustrated by Thomas Berkau

CRICKET
VISION
PRESS

**ABC Charlotte**
Text copyright ©2014 by Christina Berkau Pope
Illustrations copyright ©2014 by Thomas Berkau
First Edition 2014

Graphic Design Services by Pete Hurdle

All rights reserved.  No part of this book may be reproduced in any manner
without the express written consent of the publisher, except in the case of brief
excerpts in critical reviews and articles.  All inquiries should be addressed to:

**Cricket Vision Press**
1116 Linda Lane
Charlotte, North Carolina 28211
www.cricketvisionpress.com

**ISBN: 978-0-692-21791-7**

Display and text type set in Square Meal and Clarendon
Each illustration is hand drawn prior to adding full digital color
Printed in Korea by Pacom

This book is dedicated to BTP, the
coolest little dude we know, and
to his Nana and Papa.  Thank you
for the inspiration and endless
support!  We love you A LOT!

Welcome to Charlotte, North Carolina! What a lovely view from the sky. Look at all I discovered while flying by…

An albatross (that's me!) admiring an airplane at Carolinas Aviation Museum.

B  A basset hound basking in a foot bath at Ballantyne Spa.

 A chameleon carefully catching the hockey puck at a Charlotte Checkers game.

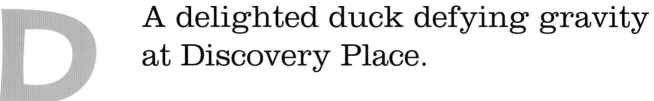 A delighted duck defying gravity at Discovery Place.

**E** An elephant enjoying some entertainment at the EPICENTRE.

 A feisty ferret playing frisbee in Freedom Park.

 A gopher grazing gracefully on The Green Uptown.

 A happy hippo hiking to the highest hilltop on Crowders Mountain.

An ibex intrigued by an
interesting book at ImaginOn.

 A jaunty jackal joining in a joust at Carolina Renaissance Festival.

 A kitschy kitten with a knack for catching fly balls at a Charlotte Knights game.

**L** A laid-back llama learning lip slides on Lake Norman.

 A monkey marveling over a masterpiece at the Mint Museum.

 A narwhal with a need for speed
at the NASCAR Hall of Fame.

 An opulent otter out for an evening at Ovens Auditorium.

P A peppy penguin displaying some
Carolina Panthers football pride.

A queen bee quickly cruising through campus at Queens University of Charlotte.

R A rhinoceros helping a resident recover at Carolina Raptor Center.

 A squid strumming strings with the Charlotte Symphony at Symphony Park.

T A touring toad riding the trolley
down Trade and Tryon Streets.

 An umbrella cockatoo unpacking
for undergrad at UNC Charlotte®.

 A vivacious vole cranking up the volume at the Visulite.

 A walrus whipping over wild waves at the U.S. National Whitewater Center.

A xolo exiting onto Interstate 77 to explore exciting Charlotte.

Y A yak yelling "Opa!" to the crowds at the Yiasou Greek Festival.

**Z** A zebra catching some zzz's after a busy day at Lazy 5 Ranch.

Thanks for joining me
in the Queen City to play
and explore!

I hope to see you again as
I travel more and more!